Johnny's Daddy had a Heart Attack

Learning about CPR from a Child's Perspective

By Patricia Policastro, RN, PCCN

Outer Banks Publishing Group
Raleigh/Outer Banks

Illustrations by Maverick Book Services
www.mavericktambiga.wixsite.com/bookservices

FIRST EDITION – May 2018

ISBN 13 - 978-1-7320452-0-0
ISBN 10 - 1-7320452-0-8
eISBN - 9781370207657

Hello, my name is Johnny. One day my Mommy, Daddy, and I went to the park for a family day.

I love to play in the playground!

My Daddy watched while Mommy and I played on the slide.

Suddenly, Daddy was sweating and breathing a lot. I saw Daddy put his hands on his chest. Mommy asked Daddy,

"What is the matter?"

Daddy said, "I am having chest pain, and I can't breathe."

Mommy took out her cell phone and said, "I will call 911."

Mommy told me 911 is the number to call when you need help for an emergency.

Daddy then laid down on the bench and went to sleep.

"Daddy, Daddy, wake up!"

Two people came. I asked Mommy who were they?

Mommy said they are called Emergency Medical Technicians or EMTs for short.

They help people with their health when you are not in a doctor's office.

While Daddy was still sleeping, they moved him off the bench.

The EMT called out to him to try to wake him while watching his chest, but Daddy didn't wake up.

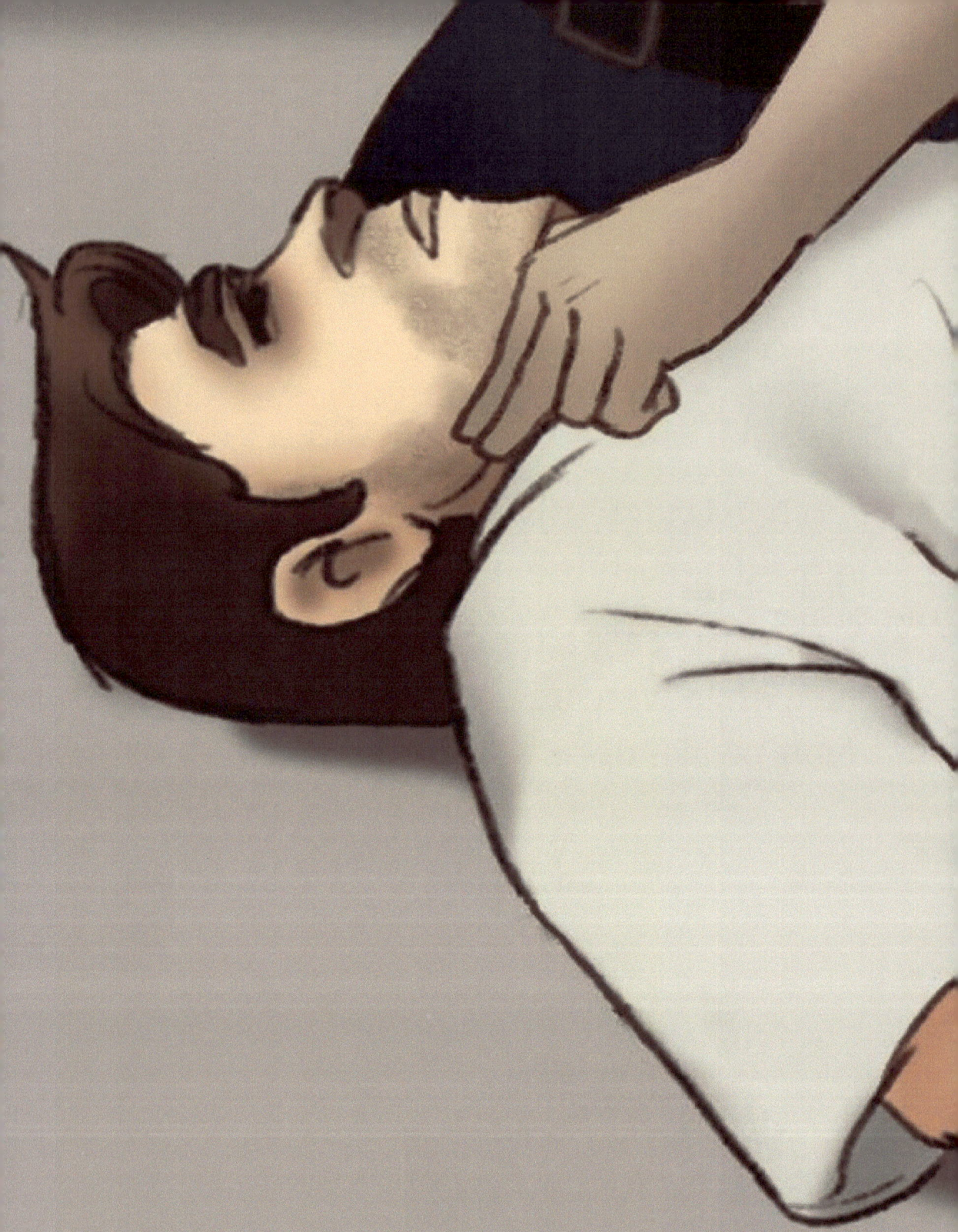

The EMT then placed two fingers on my Daddy's neck.

Mommy told me the man is checking for my Daddy's heartbeat by feeling it in the blood vessels in his neck. The blood vessels carry blood throughout his body like a hose carries water for the lawn.

The man EMT started to press on my Daddy's chest with his hands.

I told Mommy, "He will hurt Daddy!"

Mommy explained, "No honey, he is trying to help Daddy. By pressing on Daddy's chest, the EMT is pumping blood from Daddy's heart to the rest of his body. It is called CPR for short."

The girl EMT then looked like she was going to kiss Daddy and blew air into my Daddy's mouth two times by using a mask.

Mommy explained, "The girl EMT is giving Daddy air in his lungs like blowing up a balloon by using a protective mask. Your lungs and heart work together to keep you breathing. A protective mask protects the EMT from infection or getting sick."

The other EMT began to press on Daddy's chest again.

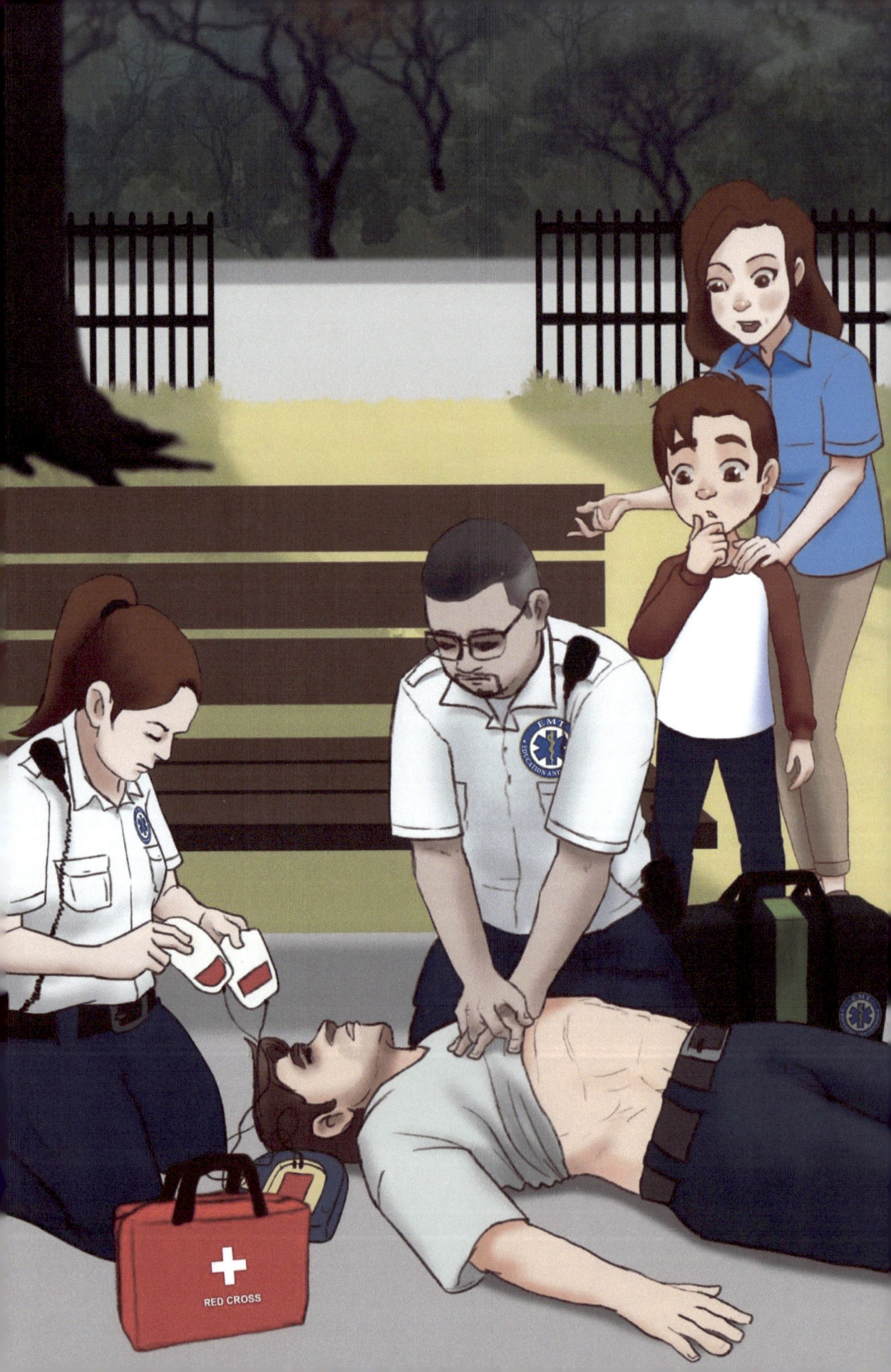

The girl EMT took out an electronic game and attached pads and wires to my Daddy's chest.

The EMT stopped pressing on Daddy's chest.

I asked Mommy, "Did the man stop helping Daddy?"

Mommy said, "No honey, now the other EMT is helping Daddy. They are taking turns. The EMT is using the electronic box to check how Daddy's heart is beating."

"What do you mean by Daddy's heart beating, Mommy?"

"Your heart has electricity which enables it to pump automatically all of the time, throughout your life," Mommy explained.

The EMT then stretched his arms out and shouted,

"Clear, all clear, everyone clear!" and then the other EMT pressed a button on the game box. I then saw my Daddy's body jump a little.

I asked Mommy, "Why is the EMT yelling? Why do we have to stay away from Daddy?"

Mommy explained, "The EMT's are yelling to keep everyone who is close to Daddy a safe distance away from him.

"The electronic box, called an AED, has electrical power that could give someone touching Daddy a shock, just like a dose of lightning. This dose of electricity could be harmful for someone who's heart is beating at a normal speed.

"Daddy's heart is beating too fast, so right now his heart needs this electricity. The electricity from the AED is designed to stop Daddy's heart beat so it can restart on its own at a normal speed. The electricity travels from the AED box, through the wires, to the pads that are on Daddy's chest."

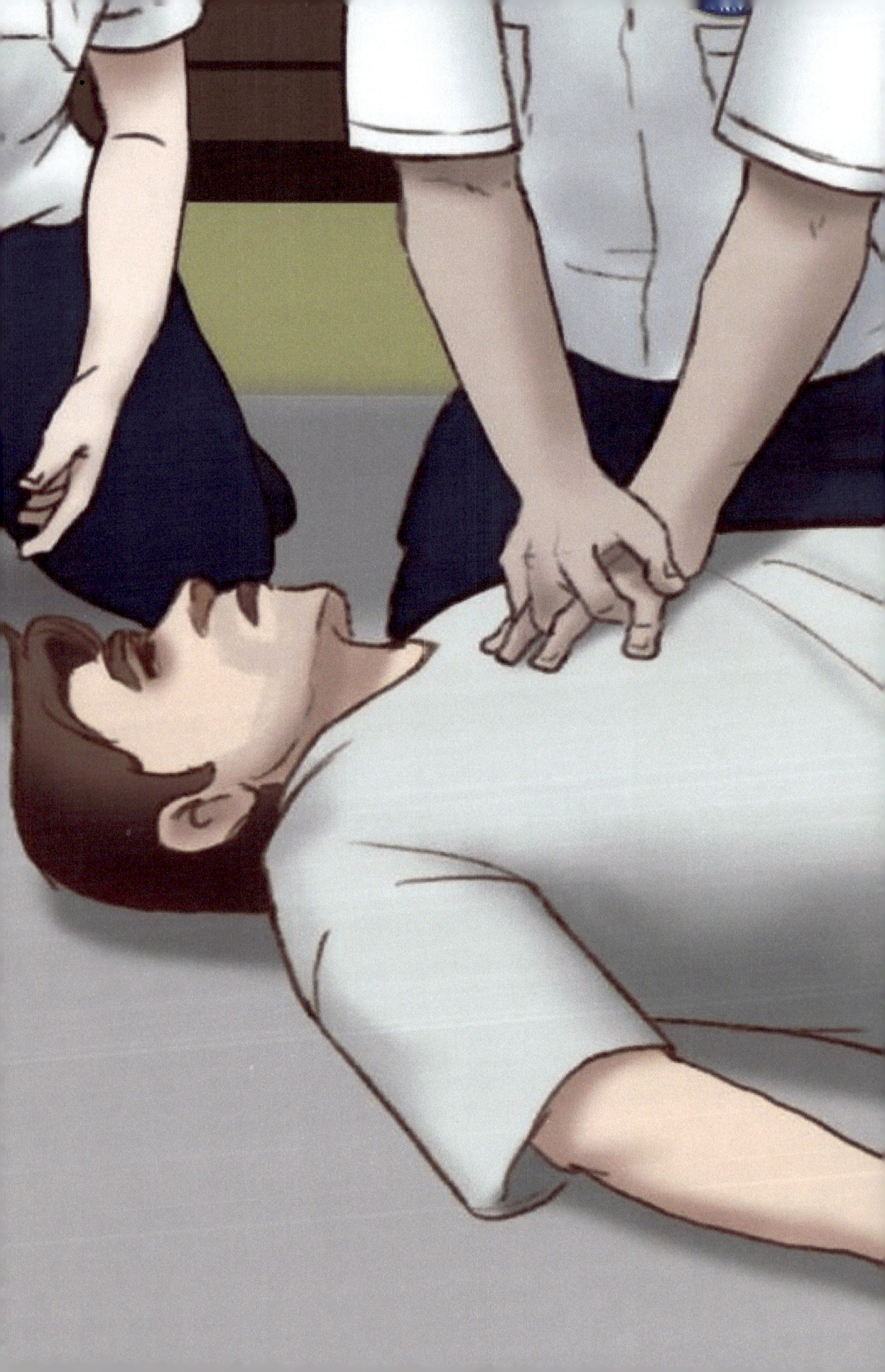

The EMT then began to press on my Daddy's chest again.

"Mommy is the EMT going to hurt Daddy!"

"No, honey, remember he is trying to help Daddy by keeping his blood pumping through his body."

Mommy helped me count the number of times the man pressed on Daddy's chest. We counted 30.

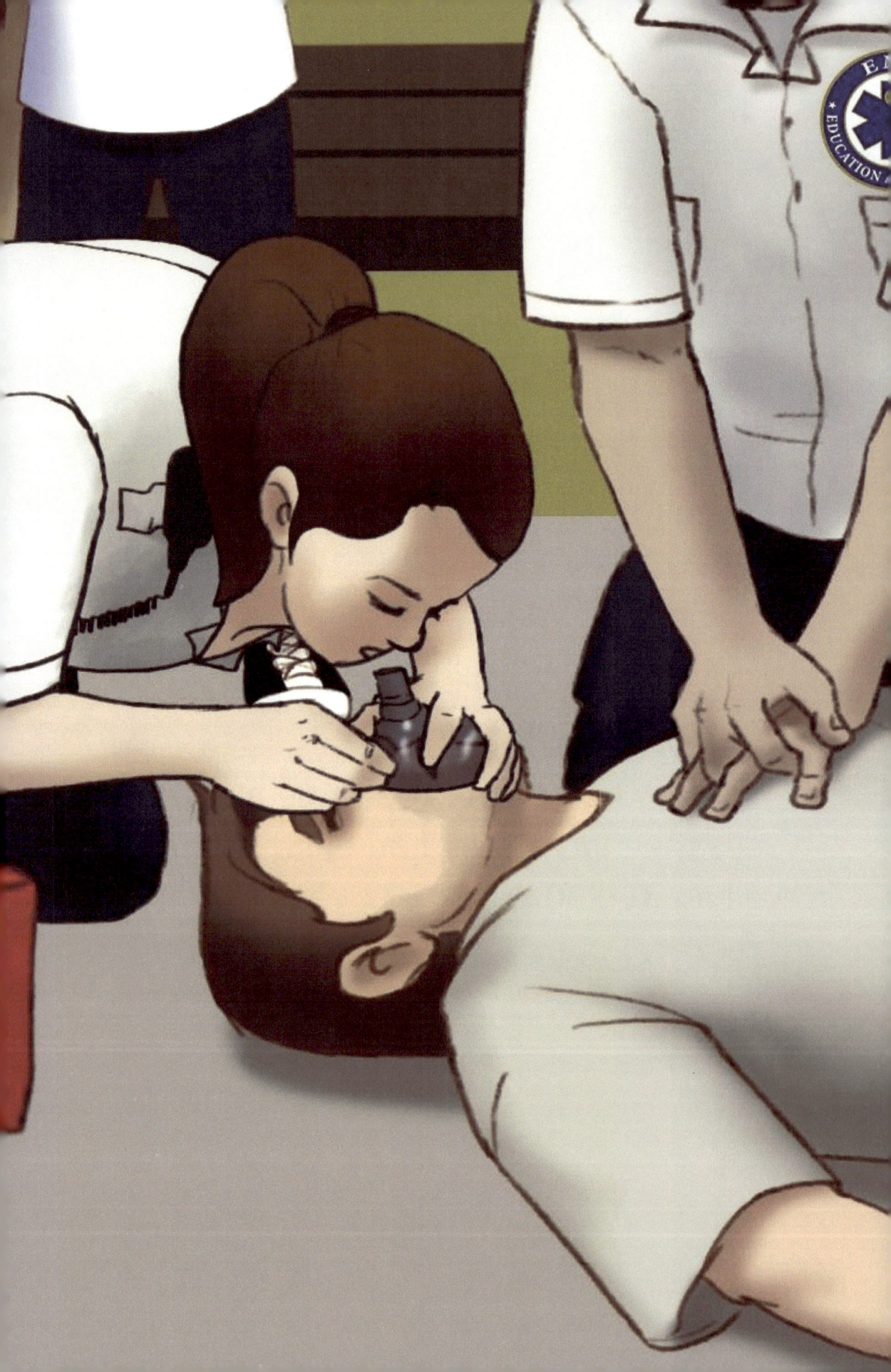

The girl EMT blew air into Daddy's mouth again; I counted two times.

"Mommy, why is it called, C?"

"Honey, it's called Cardiopulmonary Resuscitation, which is CPR for short.

"And Mommy, the box is called A?"

"It is an AED, which stands for Automated External Defibrillator. I know Johnny, these words are hard to remember and difficult to pronounce. That's why it's easier to use the short words for them."

Then the EMT placed his 2 fingers on Daddy's neck and said,

"There's a heartbeat! He is breathing and moving!"

The EMT's helped Daddy onto a stretcher, which is a bed on wheels. "Mommy told me it is called a stretcher."

They put the stretcher in an ambulance and took him to the hospital. Mommy and I followed the ambulance to the hospital in our car.

Daddy was awake when we arrived. I hugged Daddy!

Mommy began talking with Daddy's doctor. Mommy told me that Daddy would have to stay in the hospital for a few days.

Mommy said, "Staying in the hospital *isn't punishment*. It is a special place where doctors could examine Daddy more, so he gets better."

Mommy told me it is important for Daddy so he can get well.

"I will miss you Daddy, but I promise to be good for Mommy until you come home from the hospital."

The End

Message from the Author - Why I wrote this book

The purpose of this story is to teach children CPR knowledge, while hoping to also relieve their fear should they witness someone experiencing such an event. The story was inspired by a friend's husband who had a heart attack when their son was about Johnny's age. He has a history of smoking.

According to the Centers for Disease Control and Prevention, heart disease is the #1 killer of both men and women. The most common type of heart disease is coronary artery disease. Having high blood pressure, elevated cholesterol, or a history of smoking are key risk factors for heart disease. Approximately half of adult Americans have one of these risk factors.

According to the American Heart Association, bystander use of defibrillators (Automated External Defibrillator - AED) can dramatically increase the survival rate of people who experience a cardiac arrest. If a cardiac arrest occurs in a public place, the person has more than twice the chance to survive if a bystander utilizes an AED before EMT's arrive. When you are in a public place, it would be worthwhile to notice the location of an AED in case of an emergency. Most people might not be aware, AED's are simple to use. When the device is turned on, it has voice commands to instruct you, and the pads have illustrations for proper placement, which makes it easy for anyone to use.

Physical inactivity also attributes to heart disease. Children need to start learning at a young age to stay active, eat healthy, and avoid bad habits such as smoking. This type of lifestyle can lead to a healthier, longer life.

Many thanks to those who have helped create *Learning about CPR from a Child's Perspective* including Scott Larson from Safety NJ, Jason Bhulai, and Katherine Ginona, who all willingly volunteered their time to pose for the CPR photographs used to create the illustrations.

BIBLIOGRAPHY

Gibson, Karen Bush. Emergency Medical Technicians. Mankato: Bridgestone Books, 2001.

Rogers, Fred. Going To The Hospital. New York: Putnam's Sons. C1988.

Haney, Johannah. Heart Disease. New York: Benchmark Books. C2005.

Hazinski, Mary Fran, RN, MSN, ed. BLS For Healthcare Providers. USA: American Heart Association.

American Heart Association News, February 26, 2018, Bystander Use of Defibrillators Can Dramatically Boost Survival of Cardiac Arrest Patients from http://news.heart.org

The Centers for Disease Control and Prevention, National Center for Chronic Disease Prevention and Health promotion, Division for Heart Disease and Stroke Prevention, Heart Disease in the United States, Americans at Risk for Heart Disease from http://www.cdc.gov

About the Author

Patricia Policastro has been a registered nurse for 13 years and works as a Clinical Research Coordinator in a New Jersey medical center in Cardiac Research.

She is a member of the American Association of Critical-Care Nurses since 2009 and holds a certificate as a Progressive Care Certified Nurse.

She is also American Heart Association Basic Life Support and Advanced Cardiovascular Life Support certified as well.

Patricia became an RN specializing in cardiology care due to a history of cardiac disease in her family.

She lives in New Jersey and enjoys Zumba for exercise, dancing and listening to music, and bicycle rides when the weather permits. She also cherishes time spent with family and friends.

www.ingramcontent.com/pod-product-compliance
Lightning Source LLC
Chambersburg PA
CBHW042103040426

42448CB00002B/125